D0186165

A books timeline

c. 2500 BC

Cuneiform tablets produced in Mesopotamia.

868

The Diamond Sutra is published in China – the earliest surviving example of a printed book. It is a paper scroll printed from woodblocks.

c. 295 BC

The Library of Alexandria is founded, in Egypt.

1439–1450

Johannes Gutenberg develops the first movable-type printing press in Europe.

c. 2400 BCE

The date of the earliest surviving papyrus scrolls, from Egypt.

c. 1040

Bi Sheng develops movable-type printing in China.

AD 105

Vegetable-fibre paper is developed in China.

1819

William Pickering publishes his Diamond Classics, the first clothbound books, sold at a price ordinary people could afford.

1653

The first North American public library is founded, in Franklin, Massachusetts.

1998–2007

E-book readers start to gain popular appeal.

1751–1772

Denis Diderot publishes his *Encyclopédie*.

2007

The first print-on-demand machine is installed in the central branch of the New York Public Library.

1605 and 1615

Don Quixote by Miguel de Cervantes is published – widely regarded as the first modern novel.

1843

Richard Hoe invents the rotary printing press.

Gutenberg's press

Screw: *A strong wooden screw provides the pressure that forces the platen down onto the forme.*

Devil's tail: *This is the printers' nickname for the handle that turns the screw.*

Body: *The body of the press provides a stable platform for the printing process.*

Ink ball: *Ink is applied to the type by hand, using a leather ink ball.*

Forme: *Cast metal 'sorts' (letters, numerals and punctuation marks) are composited into words and lines of text and tightly bound together to make up a page image called a 'forme'. The forme is mounted on the press and then inked, ready to make an impression on paper.*

Frisket: *A second frame, made of parchment, which protects the margins of the paper from ink stains.*

Tympan: *The paper is held in a hinged frame called a tympan. This is lowered onto the printing surface and pushed beneath the screw clamp.*

Platen: *A flat wooden plate which presses the paper down onto the forme to make an impression.*

This is a reconstruction of Johannes Gutenberg's printing press (c. 1439). Presses of this type were still being built right up to the 19th century. See page 17 for a different view of the press.

NORFOLK	
LIBRARIES & INFORMATION SERVICE	
1533818	
PETERS	15-Jan-2015
681.62	£6.99
PBK	

Author:

Alex Woolf studied history at Essex University, England. He is the author of over 60 books for children, many of them on historical topics. They include *Days That Shook the World: Assassination in Sarajevo* and *Past in Pictures: A Photographic View of World War One.*

Artist:

David Antram was born in Brighton, England, in 1958. He studied at Eastbourne College of Art and then worked in advertising for 15 years before becoming a full-time artist. He has illustrated many children's non-fiction books.

Series creator:

David Salariya was born in Dundee, Scotland. He has illustrated a wide range of books and has created and designed many new series for publishers in the UK and overseas. David established The Salariya Book Company in 1989. He lives in Brighton with his wife, illustrator Shirley Willis, and their son Jonathan.

Editors: **Caroline Coleman, Stephen Haynes**

Editorial Assistant: **Mark Williams**

Published in Great Britain in MMXV by Book House, an imprint of
The Salariya Book Company Ltd
25 Marlborough Place, Brighton BN1 1UB
www.salariya.com
www.book-house.co.uk
ISBN: 978-1-910184-04-2

SALARIYA

© The Salariya Book Company Ltd MMXV
All rights reserved. No part of this publication may be reproduced, stored in or introduced into a retrieval system or transmitted in any form, or by any means (electronic, mechanical, photocopying, recording or otherwise) without the written permission of the publisher. Any person who does any unauthorised act in relation to this publication may be liable to criminal prosecution and civil claims for damages.

1 3 5 7 9 8 6 4 2

A CIP catalogue record for this book is available from the British Library.

Printed and bound in China.

This book is sold subject to the conditions that it shall not, by way of trade or otherwise, be lent, resold, hired out, or otherwise circulated without the publisher's prior consent in any form or binding or cover other than that in which it is published and without similar condition being imposed on the subsequent purchaser.

Visit our website at **www.book-house.co.uk**
or go to **www.salariya.com** for **free** electronic versions of:
You Wouldn't Want to be an Egyptian Mummy!
You Wouldn't Want to be a Roman Gladiator!
You Wouldn't Want to be a Polar Explorer!
You Wouldn't Want to sail on a 19th-Century Whaling Ship!

**PAPER FROM
SUSTAINABLE
FORESTS**

You Wouldn't Want to Live Without™ Books!

Written by
Alex Woolf

Illustrated by
David Antram

Created and designed by
David Salariya

BOOK HOUSE
a SALARIYA *imprint*

Contents

Introduction

What exactly is a book? According to the dictionary, it's a written or printed work made up of pages glued or sewn together along one side and bound in covers. Well, that may be what modern books look like, but books have existed in other forms as well. It would be more accurate to say that a book is an object designed to be read with the purpose of spreading information, ideas, stories and entertainment to many different people.

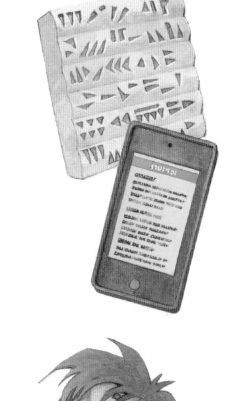

Books have been around for thousands of years, although they looked a bit different back then. And they may look different in the future, too – the book is still developing in new and exciting ways. In this (paper and ink) book, we trace the history of books from their earliest origins as clay tablets to their very latest incarnation – the e-book. We'll learn how important they've been to our culture and civilisation and how we really, really, wouldn't want to live without them.

Are you ready to write?

Imagine living in a world before writing. All communication is by speech, which means you can only exchange news and information with the people immediately around you. The world beyond your village is a mystery. You don't know anything about the past either, except through stories passed down from your parents – and those stories seem to change with each retelling.

But one day, you're wandering near another village when you come across a piece of tree bark with some mysterious patterns carved into its surface. Looking closer, they seem like little pictures. You think to yourself: what if each of these patterns means something…?

I'm sure he told it differently last week.

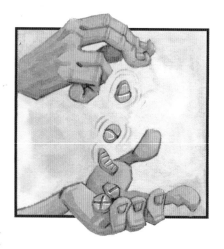

COUNTING TOKENS. The first kind of writing wasn't words, but numbers. Early farmers needed a way of recording things like how much land or livestock they had.

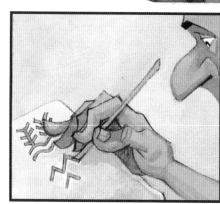

PICTURE WRITING. Around 5,000 years ago, people began using pictures, known as glyphs, to represent objects or ideas.

We still use picture symbols today. What emotions are these faces expressing? Try creating picture symbols for some other emotions.

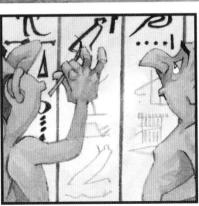

WRITING WORDS. The next development was to use symbols, called logograms, to represent words. This linked written language with spoken language.

ALPHABETS. Signs started to be used to represent the sounds of speech. These signs, or letters, were put together to form words. A set of letters is an alphabet.

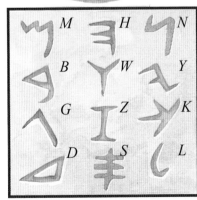

Phoenician alphabet, c. 1050 BC

7

Could you carve your text on a tablet?

You are a scribe living in Mesopotamia around 2500 BC. As one of the first writers, you need something to write *on*. You use tablets – and we're not talking electronics here! These tablets are made of clay, and you carve words into their surface using a blunt reed. This writing style is called *cuneiform*, meaning 'wedge-shaped'. It is easy to make impressions in the soft clay surface. And when the tablets are baked, the marks become permanent. Just don't make a mistake before you bake!

10th–11th centuries AD

How dare you!

5th century BC

STURDY STONE. The Vikings carved letters onto stone tablets (right). This took time and effort, but left marks that would last for centuries.

ADISTEIDE
KIMDN. MIATIAΩ

ANCIENT GREEKS wrote on broken pieces of pottery called *ostraka* (left and above). Citizens would write the name of the person they thought should be exiled. From this we get the word *ostracism*.

8th century BC and later

WAX TABLETS. The Greeks and Romans also wrote on wooden tablets covered with a layer of wax, using a pointed tool called a stylus (left and below).

WOODEN STRIPS. The main writing materials in early China were wood or bamboo strips on which characters were painted (right).

c. 1250 BC–4th century AD

Cuneiform tablet from ancient Mesopotamia, c. 2500 BC

You can do it!

To make a clay tablet, flatten a lump of clay, then cut off the end of a lolly stick to make a straight edge for wedge-shaped writing. Mark some cuneiform characters on the clay surface.

That should be 79 cattle, not 78. Do it again!

Wouldn't it be easier just to eat one cow?

Are you prepared for papyrus?

Imagine you're a scribe living 4,000 years ago in ancient Egypt. You're feeling frustrated. Stone tablets are all very well, but they're heavy! There's not a lot of room on their surface, and you can't correct your mistakes. Then, one day, a friend shows you a new material called papyrus, made from a type of reed. Papyrus is light, thin and flexible, and comes in long sheets that can be rolled up. The juice of the reed, mixed with soot, makes ink, which you can use to write on the papyrus. It's fantastic! Your days of lugging around stone tablets are over!

Making papyrus

SLICE the stalks into thin strips, soak in water, roll them flat and leave them to dry.

PLACE the strips side by side, then lay a second set at right angles to the first.

POUND the sheet to drain excess water. The plant's own sap helps the layers stick together.

AFTER DRYING under a stone, polish the surface smooth using shell or ivory.

Say what you like about stone, at least we had to keep it brief.

You can do it!

To make a scroll, soak a sheet of paper in tea for an hour to turn it brown. Let it dry, then roll up the paper from one end. Secure with a piece of string. If you prefer, you could tape a chopstick to each end of the sheet before rolling it up towards the centre from both sides.

What are you making?

Shhh! Don't tell him.

PAPER was invented by the Chinese in AD 105 or earlier. They kept it secret until 751, when an Arab army captured some Chinese papermakers.

IN THE 1ST CENTURY BC, a new writing surface emerged in Europe: parchment, made from animal skins. Unlike papyrus, it didn't rot in damp conditions, and could be scraped clean and reused.

SCROLLS. With the development of flexible writing surfaces, books could be much longer. For convenience, they were rolled up to form scrolls.

Why not curl up with a codex?

As a Christian living in the second century AD, you think scrolls are great, but you have to admit they can be tricky to handle. Some are over 10 metres long, and you can waste a lot of time trying to find the particular bit of holy scripture you're interested in. Wouldn't it be more convenient to fold a stack of sheets in half and glue them together on one side to make individual pages? You could even put boards around the pages for protection. The codex, as this new invention is called, is so much easier to handle than a scroll.

It'll never catch on.

SIMPLE, BUT BRILLIANT. The codex was more compact than a scroll, and both sides of the paper could be used. You could even add page numbers and have an index.

> I came, I saw, I, er... wrote about it.

ORIGINS.
No-one knows who invented the codex. Some believe it was Roman emperor Julius Caesar, who apparently turned his scrolls into a notebook for convenience.

How it works

Concertina books are made by dividing a long sheet of paper into page widths, then folding back and forth along these divisions. Boards may be glued to the end pages for protection.

PALM-LEAF TEXTS. While the codex was being invented in the West, Buddhists in the East were writing sacred texts on dried palm leaves, bound together with string and secured between wooden boards (left).

THE CONCERTINA BOOK, or *orihon* (below), was developed in China and Japan in the 800s AD.

Could you be a scribe in a scriptorium?

You are a monk in 9th-century Europe. You work in the scriptorium (writing room) of the monastery, copying religious works in Latin, Greek or Hebrew. You don't understand much of what you write, but no matter, so long as your work is neat and reasonably accurate – though even the best scribes make at least one mistake per page. You're expected to copy three to four pages a day, working only in daylight hours, because candles are expensive, and a fire risk.

Curtain tied back to let in light

Knife used to sharpen quills and scrape away mistakes

Lectern: angled writing board so ink doesn't flow out too fast

Quill pen

Footstool to protect your feet from the cold stone floor

Ink pots: black for text, red and blue for headings

LIBRARIES have existed since 2600 BC. The most famous in the ancient world was the Library of Alexandria in Egypt. It was destroyed by fire c. AD 273.

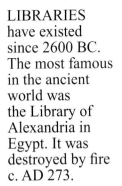

First, the scribe ruled accurate lines on the parchment page. Then the text was written in, leaving gaps for the illuminated letters, which were put in later by a painter. Sometimes the scribe left notes for the painter in the margin.

IN MEDIEVAL EUROPE, libraries were maintained by monasteries. The most valuable books were chained to the shelves.

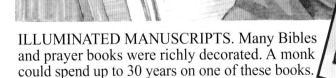

ILLUMINATED MANUSCRIPTS. Many Bibles and prayer books were richly decorated. A monk could spend up to 30 years on one of these books.

BOOK OF KELLS. This extraordinary book of the Gospels was created by 9th-century Irish monks and is made up of 340 lavishly illustrated pages.

Can you feel the power of print?

Only 499 pages to go!

It is 1439. You are Johannes Gutenberg, a jeweller and metalworker based in Strasbourg, on the border between France and Germany. There's a growing demand for books, but they're expensive and time-consuming to produce. One day, you have an idea: a machine with individual metal letters that could be lined up to form blocks of text. The letters could be covered in ink and pressed onto paper. Thanks to your invention – the movable-type printing press – books could be mass-produced, helping to spread learning to ordinary people.

WOODBLOCK PRINTING. Printing existed in Europe before Gutenberg. People would carve letters into a block of wood, cover it in ink and press it onto paper. However, a new block of wood had to be carved for each page.

I could have written that in a year.

Yes, but I printed 180.

CHINA WAS FIRST. A printer named Bi Sheng invented the world's first movable-type system around AD 1040.

TYPESETTING. Compositors set the type. They assembled the characters by hand in a composing stick.

GUTENBERG'S BIBLE. In about 1450, Gutenberg started work on a Bible. It took him two years to typeset and print.

MOVABLE-TYPE PRINTING PRESS. Gutenberg based his press on screw presses used in olive oil and wine production. The great advantage of movable type was that you could change the letters around to form new words when a new page was required.

For more information on how the press works, see the drawing near the front of the book.

Body

Screw

Handle or 'devil's tail'

Tympan (with forme underneath)

Platen

Bed

You can do it!

You can make a block print from any easily carvable surface, such as soap. Write your initial in mirror image on the surface, then carve away everything apart from the letter. Spread ink on the letter, and press down on some paper.

One day they'll write books about me.

Yes, and they'll print them, too!

17

Are you feeling enlightened?

As a young student living in Paris in the year 1789, you are a regular at the salons and coffee houses where you converse with other intellectuals. Paris is at the centre of a movement called the Enlightenment. Its aim is to reform society using reason. You have read all the latest books and pamphlets, and are inspired by their ideas about equality and freedom. They also make you angry about the wealth and power of the king and the nobility. One of these days you're sure there's going to be a revolution!

CHEEKY CHAPBOOKS. Those who couldn't afford books bought cheaply made pamphlets called 'chapbooks' (right). Many contained fairytales, comic stories, romances, songs, recipes and horoscopes.

I disagree!

Down with the king!

It says so here.

Why?

I can read while I work!

BOOKS AND REVOLUTION. Printing allowed new ideas to spread more rapidly. This was one cause of the French Revolution, which broke out in 1789.

NEW READERS. Printing also made books cheaper, helping literacy spread among ordinary people.

Reading a chapbook

ENORMOUS *ENCYCLOPÉDIE*. One of the greatest products of the Enlightenment was the encyclopaedia edited by Denis Diderot. It was published in 28 volumes between 1751 and 1772.

Top tip

Pamphlets are printed booklets, consisting of a few pages folded in half and stapled. Is there an issue you feel passionate about? Why not try writing down your ideas in a pamphlet?

Listen to me, everybody!

Hear, hear!

Could you be a pioneer of publishing?

t is 1824. You have just opened one of the very first publishing houses that isn't also a printer. Due to the rising demand for books, the businesses of printing and publishing have become separated. As a publisher, you know very little about printing, but a great deal about readers and the kinds of books they're interested in. You must decide how much to pay your authors, how much to charge for your books, and how to get them to your readers.

We can pay you a royalty of 10%.

He always wanted to get into print.

MECHANISED PRINTING. By 1900, steam-powered rotary presses could produce 48,000 pages per hour.

LINOTYPE MACHINE. Compositors entered text on a keyboard and this was then automatically assembled into lines of type.

RISE OF THE NOVEL. By the 1800s, many people had time to read and money to buy books. Novelists like Charles Dickens (above) became hugely popular.

That means for every book sold, you get one tenth of the profit.

To make a paperback, clamp the long edge of a stack of loose sheets with a bulldog clip. Apply PVA glue to the other side (the spine). Take a piece of thin card the size of two of the pages plus the spine. Score two folds where the cover will fold around the spine, then carefully fit the cover around the pages.

BOOKS FOR ALL. From the mid-19th century, publishers began to mass-produce cheap paper-bound editions of popular works. The paperback really took off in 1935 with the launch of Penguin Books.

No, I was just asking the price.

To Emma Chissett?

BOOKSHOPS. During the 19th century, publishing and bookselling separated. Bookshops and bookstalls opened in many towns and cities.

LIBRARIES. By 1845, people could borrow books for free from public lending libraries.

Do you think books are dangerous?

It is the night of 10 May 1933. You are a schoolchild in Nazi Germany. A large and noisy crowd marches by in a torchlight parade. You follow them to the town square, where they start hurling books onto a giant bonfire. A band plays and the crowd sing songs as the books crackle and burn. A Nazi official gives a speech. 'These books corrupt the minds of those who read them,' he says. 'They are dangerous.'

You watch the books ignite. You imagine the ink of those 'dangerous' words melting away, and you wonder: how exactly can a book be dangerous?

For as long as there have been books, there have been people – usually powerful people – who want to stop others reading them. Why? Because they fear the ideas books contain and the effect these ideas may have on those who read them.

ANCIENT CHINESE EMPEROR Qin Shi Huang not only burned books, he also buried alive 460 scholars (left).

THE MEDIEVAL CHURCH believed the Bible should only be read in Latin, so Church leaders burned copies of William Tyndale's English translation (right). Tyndale himself was burnt at the stake in 1536.

THE RULERS of 18th-century France frequently sent the books they didn't like, as well as their authors, to the Bastille, a prison fortress in Paris (left).

DR THOMAS BOWDLER (1754–1825) produced a version of Shakespeare's plays that left out anything he thought unsuitable for women and children. Nowadays, a 'bowdlerised' book is one made worse through censorship.

It doesn't seem right to burn Bibles.

I sentence you...

Could you survive as a self-publisher?

It is 1984. You decide to write, design and illustrate your own book, using nothing more than a personal computer. The technology to do this has just come onto the market. It's called desktop publishing (DTP). With DTP, you can create professional-looking books in your own home. And, as printing becomes cheaper, people like you will soon be able to afford to print their own books, too. Now everyone can be a publisher!

PRINT-ON-DEMAND technology, which emerged in the early 2000s, offers self-published authors the opportunity to print and deliver single copies of a book each time one is ordered. No need for a warehouse to store all those unsold copies!

But it can't write books yet!

BREAKING RECORDS. In 2008, for the first time in history, more books were self-published than published traditionally. But will readers be confused by so much choice?

THE WRITE STUFF. One of the functions of a publisher is to seek out the most talented authors. But, if anyone can publish a book, how do readers know which books are good?

Will you welcome the World Wide Web?

t is 2006. Your bookshop is struggling to survive. These days, many people prefer to buy their books from online retailers. They're open 24/7, offer customer reviews of their books, and you can't compete with them on price. The Internet has also made it harder to sell reference books. If people want to look up a fact, they search online. So what can you do? Well, why not use the Internet to your advantage? Start a blog, get active on social media, raise awareness of your bookshop. Host regular events for the local community. Before long, your shop starts getting busy again.

TWO for ONE

Here already? That was quick!

CUSTOMER CONVENIENCE: Today, you can buy a book with a simple click of the mouse. You can read reviews and sometimes sample a few pages before buying. Also, online bookshops are usually open 24 hours a day. What would Dickens have thought?

SUSPECT SOURCES. The Internet has changed the way we access information. Instead of getting facts from books, we look them up online. The trouble is, if anyone can post information, how can we trust it?

I don't know who to believe...

You can do it!

We have a yoga class, a knitting club... Oh yes, we sell books as well.

Why not join an online book discussion group for people your age, or even start your own? Next time you read a book, write a review and post it on the group's website.

BUY 1 GET 1 FREE!

THANKS TO SOCIAL MEDIA and blogging, anyone can potentially become a bestselling author.

Be the first to review my new book, out next Thursday!

How does the story end?

Don't rush me, I'm still thinking!

WEB FICTION. Some authors now publish their books online instead of on paper. You can download each chapter as soon as the author has written it.

Is life easier with an e-book?

It's the present day. You've just bought your first e-book reader. It's easy on the eyes, not like reading off a computer screen. You can look up words you don't understand simply by clicking on them. You can adjust the size of the type, and make notes about what you've read. You can link to the Internet to buy new e-books. You can store an entire library on one slim piece of plastic – wonderful!

But does this mean printed books are finished? Will they go the way of the scroll and the handwritten codex? You don't think so. Not yet, anyway.

ENHANCED E-BOOKS. Some e-books have interactive features to enhance readers' enjoyment of the stories, such as audio or video commentaries from the author, music and sound effects.

AUGMENTED REALITY. AR books, when placed in front of a webcam, create sounds and 3-D animation effects on your computer screen.

SOCIAL READING. E-books allow us to share our opinions on books with others and follow other people's comments. Reading can be a sociable activity.

FROM TABLET TO TABLET. Books have changed over time. But, whether made of clay or plastic, their function is the same: to educate, inform and entertain.

Glossary

Blog A website or web page on which a person can write about what they're interested in and link to other sites.

Chapbook A pamphlet containing tales, ballads, prayers and other short works, sold by peddlers (chapmen).

Codex A handwritten work in the form of pages glued or sewn together at one side and bound in a cover.

Composing stick A tool used to assemble pieces of metal type into words and lines ready for printing. The person who uses it is a **compositor**.

Cuneiform An ancient form of writing consisting of wedge-shaped characters impressed on a clay tablet.

Desktop publishing (DTP) The creation of books by laying out pages on a personal computer.

Enlightenment A European movement of the late 17th and 18th centuries, which stated that it was better to live by reason than to follow tradition.

French Revolution A period of radical social and political upheaval in France, from 1789 to 1799.

Glyph A picture, character or symbol representing an object or idea.

Illuminated manuscript A medieval manuscript ornamented with miniature illustrations, borders and decorated initial letters.

Lectern A book stand with a sloping top, used for reading or writing.

Linotype A typesetting machine. The operator entered text on a keyboard, and the machine then assembled lines of words on strips of metal for printing.

Logogram A sign or character representing a word.

Manuscript A handwritten book or document.

Mesopotamia The area between the rivers Tigris and Euphrates, roughly equivalent to present-day Iraq.

Monastery The home of a community of monks.

Movable type A printing system using separate characters that can be assembled and reassembled to make pages of text.

Nazi party The political party that governed Germany from 1933 to 1945.

Online retailer A business that sells products over the Internet.

Ostracism Banishment.

Print on demand A form of printing in which new copies of a book are not printed until an order has been received.

Quill A pen made from a main wing or tail feather of a large bird.

Reference book A book, such as a dictionary or encyclopaedia, containing information that can be found quickly when needed.

Rotary press A press that prints from a rotating cylindrical surface onto paper pressed against it by another cylinder.

Royalty Money paid to an author for each copy of a book sold.

Salon A meeting of intellectuals at the home of a fashionable society person.

Scribe A person who copies books or documents by hand.

Scriptorium A room in a monastery where manuscripts were copied.

Social media Websites and applications used to socialise online.

Typesetting Arranging type to make it ready for printing.

World Wide Web A system of linked pages within the Internet that allows users to search for information by moving from one document to another.

Index

Top ten bestselling books of all time

This list of bestsellers does not include religious texts such as the Bible, the Qur'an and the Book of Mormon. They are among the most printed books of all time, but they are often given out free, rather than sold. Mao Tse-tung's Little Red Book is not a religious text, but it, too, was distributed free.

How many have you read?

Author and title	Approximate sales
1. Miguel de Cervantes, *Don Quixote*	500 million
2. *Xinhua Zidian* (Chinese language dictionary)	400 million
3. Charles Dickens, *A Tale of Two Cities*	200 million
4. J. R. R. Tolkien, *The Lord of the Rings*	150 million
5. Antoine de Saint-Exupéry, *The Little Prince*	140 million
6. J. K. Rowling, *Harry Potter and the Philosopher's Stone**	107 million
7. Agatha Christie, *And Then There Were None*	100 million
8. Cao Xueqin, *Dream of the Red Chamber*	100 million
9. J. R. R. Tolkien, *The Hobbit*	100 million
10. C. S. Lewis, *The Lion, the Witch and the Wardrobe*	85 million

* called Sorcerer's Stone *in some countries*

The development of the printed book

Early printed books looked very similar to hand-copied manuscripts. They always opened with a richly decorated frontispiece, often followed by an engraved portrait of the author. And they usually had enormously long titles that were almost like a list of contents. Most did not have page numbers – readers were expected to add these themselves. Some printers rarely used paragraph breaks, so readers were faced with two columns of dense, unbroken text.

By the 16th century, books began to look more like their modern equivalents, with simpler opening pages and shorter titles. The introduction of page numbers, running heads and indexes helped readers to find their way around books. In the 18th century, new and clearer typefaces were designed by printers such as John Baskerville and William Caslon, helping to make texts easier to read. Typefaces based on these are still popular today.

Illustrated books

For the first 400 years of the book printing industry, text and illustrations were produced in separate workshops by completely different processes.

The earliest technique for producing book illustrations was woodblock printing. Steel engraving, invented in 1792 by Jacob Perkins, allowed sharper definition and finer detail. It was only with the invention of lithography by Alois Senefelder in 1798 that text and illustration printing could be combined on a single printing plate. A process called photogravure, developed in the 1830s, allowed photographs to be printed in books.

Did you know?

- The word *book* comes from the Danish word *bog*, meaning 'birch tree', as the early people of Denmark wrote on birch bark.

- The world's largest library is the Library of Congress in Washington, DC (USA), which contains 36 million books supported on 1,349 km of shelves.

- The world's busiest novelist is José Carlos Ryoki de Alpoim Inoue of Brazil, who published 1,058 novels between 1986 and 1996.

- The largest first print run for any book was 6.8 million copies, for J. K. Rowling's *Harry Potter and the Order of the Phoenix*.

- The world's slowest-selling book was Oxford University Press's translation of the New Testament from Coptic (a language related to ancient Egyptian) into Latin. Five hundred copies were printed in 1716 and the last one was purchased in 1907.

- The highest price ever paid for a children's book was £1.95 million, for a handwritten copy of J. K. Rowling's *The Tales of Beedle the Bard*.

Answers to the questions on page 23:
1. Galileo Galilei (1564–1642)
2. Charles Darwin (1809–1882)
3. Albert Einstein (1879–1955)